BASED ON THE FEATURE FILM PRODUCED BY MARK BURNETT AND ROMA DOWNEY

SON OF GOD

THE LIFE OF JESUS IN YOU

#1 NEW YORK TIMES BEST-SELLING AUTHOR OF *THE PURPOSE DRIVEN LIFE*

RICK WARREN

B&H
Every WORD Matters™
BHPublishingGroup.com
Nashville, Tennessee

www.ShareSonofGod.com
www.RickWarren.org

Published by B&H Publishing Group®
Copyright ©2014 RKW Legacy Partners and LightWorkers Media

ISBN: 978-1-4300-3528-2
Item: 005683780

Dewey decimal classication Number: 232.901
Subject heading: JESUS CHRIST--BIOGRAPHY \ GOD \ BIBLE. N.T. GOSPELS

TABLE OF CONTENTS

SMALL-GROUP SESSIONS

SESSION ONE

Jesus' Baptism and Your Baptism

6

SESSION TWO

Jesus' Temptation and Your Temptation

14

SESSION THREE

Jesus' Suffering and Your Suffering

22

SESSION FOUR

Jesus' Death and Your Death

30

SESSION FIVE

Jesus' Resurrection and Your Resurrection

38

SESSION SIX

Jesus' Ministry and Your Ministry

46

SMALL-GROUP RESOURCES

A NOTE TO SMALL-GROUP HOSTS

This video-based study is designed to be used with a small group of friends at home, at work, or at a church. If you're not already in a small group, start one of your own! It's easy.

How to Start a Small Group

You don't have to be a teacher. You don't need any formal training. You don't even need any experience in a small group. Just keep these four things in mind, and you'll succeed as a small-group H.O.S.T.:

Have a heart for people.

Open your home to a group of friends who want to study with you.

Serve them a snack.

Turn on the video. The six video sessions by Rick Warren provide the teaching for each session of study.

If you can do those four things, you can host a small group of your own. All of the material and instructions you need are provided in this study guide. There's no experience necessary, so enjoy the journey!

The study guide material is meant to be your servant, not your master. So please don't feel pressured to discuss every question in every session. Feel free to select the questions that seem right for your group. The point is not to race through the sessions; the point is to take time to let God work in your lives. Nor is it necessary to "go around the circle" before you move on to the next question. Give people the freedom to speak, but don't insist on it. Your group will enjoy deeper, more open sharing and discussion if people don't feel pressured to speak up.

For more information and advice on hosting a small group, see the Helps for Hosts section on page 53-55.

UNDERSTANDING YOUR STUDY GUIDE

Here is a brief explanation of the features of this workbook.

CHECKING IN: Open each meeting by briefly discussing a question or two that will help focus everyone's attention on the subject of the lesson.

KEY VERSE: Each week you will find a key Bible verse for your group to memorize together. If someone in the group has a different translation, ask them to read it aloud so the group can get a bigger picture of the meaning of the passage.

VIDEO LESSON: There is a video lesson for the group to watch together each week. Fill in the blanks in the lesson outlines as you watch the video and be sure to refer back to these outlines during your discussion time.

DISCOVERY QUESTIONS: Each video segment is complemented by several questions for group discussion. Please don't feel pressured to discuss every single question. There is no reason to rush through the answers. Give everyone ample opportunity to share their thoughts. If you don't get through all of the discovery questions, that's okay.

PUTTING IT INTO PRACTICE: We don't want to be just hearers of the Word. We also need to be doers of the Word. This section of the study contains application exercises that will help your group apply the things you are learning.

PRAYER DIRECTION: At the end of each session you will find suggestions for your group prayer time. Praying together is one of the greatest privileges of small-group life. Please don't take it for granted.

DIVING DEEPER: This section contains recommended Bible passages for your daily quiet time that will deepen your understanding of Jesus' life.

SMALL-GROUP RESOURCES: There are additional small-group resources, such as Small-Group Guidelines, Helps for Hosts, Prayer and Praise Reports, etc., in the back of this study guide.

SESSION 1

JESUS' BAPTISM
AND
YOUR BAPTISM

ⅠⅠⅠⅠⅠ CATCHING UP

Be sure to introduce everyone in your group and welcome newcomers. Review the Small-Group Guidelines on page 58 of your study guide.

• **What do you hope to get out of this study of "The Life of Christ in You"?**

_____

_____

_____

_____

_____

_____

ⅠⅠⅠⅠⅠ KEY VERSE

We were therefore buried with him through baptism into death in order that, just as Christ was raised from the dead through the glory of the Father, we too may live a new life.

ROMANS 6:4, NIV

ⅠⅠⅠⅠⅠ **WATCH** the video lesson now and take notes in your outline.

Jesus' Baptism and Your Baptism

> Then Jesus came from Galilee to the Jordan to be baptized
> by John. But John tried to deter him, saying, "I need to be
> baptized by you, and do you come to me?" Jesus replied,
> "Let it be so now; it is proper for us to do this to fulfill all
> righteousness." Then John consented. As soon as Jesus was
> baptized, he went up out of the water. At that moment heaven
> was opened, and he saw the Spirit of God descending like
> a dove and lighting on him. And a voice from heaven said,
> "This is my Son, whom I love; with him I am well pleased."
>
> **MATTHEW 3:13-17, NIV**

steped out into His ministry

God the said the same thing about us.

John the Baptist baptized people as a sign of their repentance for their sins. But Jesus had no sin. So why was Jesus baptized? It's because Jesus' baptism was His way of identifying with sinful humanity. Just as Jesus did not die for His own sins, He was not baptized for His own sins either. But in His baptism, Jesus was showing us a way to live.

Jesus said, "I didn't come to abolish the law but to fulfill it" (Matthew 5:17). In the same way, He didn't come to abolish baptism, but to fulfill it and to give it its complete meaning, which is death to sin and the old way of life, and resurrection into a new way of life.

> We died to sin; how can we live in it any longer? Or don't
> you know that all of us who were baptized into Christ
> Jesus were baptized into his death? We were therefore
> buried with him through baptism into death in order
> that, just as Christ was raised from the dead through
> the glory of the Father, we too may live a new life.
>
> **ROMANS 6:2-4, NIV**

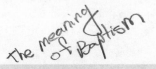

the meaning of Baptism

> Anyone who belongs to Christ has become a new person. The old life is gone; a new life has begun!
> **2 CORINTHIANS 5:17, NLT**

- **You need to be baptized because Jesus** *demonstrated* **it.**

By His own baptism, Jesus was saying, "If you truly want to follow me, then you need to follow me into this water. If I need to do this, then so do you."

- **You need to be baptized because Jesus** *commanded* **it.**

> Go and make disciples of all nations, baptizing them in the name of the Father and of the Son and of the Holy Spirit.
> **MATTHEW 28:19, NIV**

Baptism is not an option. It is a commandment for every follower of Jesus Christ.

> We know that we have come to know
> him if we obey his commands.
> **1 JOHN 2:3, NIV**

- **Baptism is your** *public statement* **that you belong to Jesus Christ.**

Your baptism tells the world that you are not ashamed to be a follower of Jesus.

> Philip began with [the] Scripture and told him the good news about Jesus. As they traveled along the road, they came to some water and the man said, "Look! Here is water. Why shouldn't I be baptized?" Philip said, "If you believe with all your heart, you may." The man answered, "I believe that Jesus Christ is the Son of God." ... Then [they] went down into the water and Philip baptized him.
>
> **ACTS 8:35-38, NIV**

- **Baptism is a symbol of** _incorporation_ .

Your baptism says you're not just a believer, you're also a belonger.

> For we were all baptized by one Spirit into one body ... Now you are the body of Christ, and each one of you is a part of it.
>
> **1 CORINTHIANS 12:13,27, NIV**

> For God so loved the world that he gave his only begotten Son, that whoever believes in him should not perish but have everlasting life.
>
> **JOHN 3:16, NKJV**

> If you confess with your mouth, 'Jesus is Lord,' and believe in your heart that God raised him from the dead, you will be saved.
>
> **ROMANS 10:9, NIV**

Discovery Questions

Feel free to select the questions that seem right for your group. There is no reason to rush through the answers. Give everyone ample opportunity to share their thoughts. If you don't get through all of the discovery questions, that's okay.

When did you accept Jesus Christ as your Savior? Where were you when you made that decision? If you haven't yet made that decision, how can this group help you?

_____

_____

_____

Have you been baptized since you made your personal decision to place your faith in Jesus Christ? If you have, share the story of your baptism with your small group.

_____

_____

_____

What does your baptism mean to you?

_____

_____

_____

Choose the verse in this lesson that is the most meaningful to you. Why did you choose that verse?

_____

_____

_____

Putting It Into Practice

If you have not been baptized since you accepted Jesus Christ as your Savior, make a plan now to be baptized like Jesus was as soon as possible. Be sure to invite your group to attend your baptism service so they can celebrate with you.

Before your next group meeting, see if you can memorize the verse you selected that was the most meaningful to you in this lesson.

Prayer Direction

Pray for your group's prayer requests. Be sure to record their requests on the Prayer and Praise Report on pages 60-61.

Diving Deeper

For your daily quiet time this week, read the following Scripture passages about Jesus' baptism.

Matthew 3:1-17; Mark 1:9-11; Luke 3:21-22; John 1:19-34

NOTES

SESSION 2
JESUS' TEMPTATION
AND
YOUR TEMPTATION

‖‖‖ CATCHING UP

- In this session we're going to talk about the importance of memorizing Scripture. Did anyone memorize the verse you selected in session one? Did you find it easy or difficult? Were you able to use the verse for your own or someone else's encouragement during the week?

_____

_____

_____

_____

_____

_____

‖‖‖ KEY VERSE

God is faithful. He will keep the temptation from
becoming so strong that you can't stand up
against it. When you are tempted, he will show you
a way out so that you will not give in to it.

1 CORINTHIANS 10:13, NLT

‖‖‖ WATCH the video lesson now and take notes in your outline.

Jesus' Temptation and Your Temptation

- It is not a _____sin_____ to be tempted.

> [Jesus] has been tempted in every way,
> just as we are—yet was without sin.
> **HEBREWS 4:15, NIV**

> Because he himself suffered when he was tempted,
> he is able to help those who are being tempted.
> **HEBREWS 2:18, NIV**

- You will never ____out grow____ temptation.

Temptation is not a sign of weakness. It is a sign that you are a threat to the Devil.

- After a spiritual ____high____, you can expect a spiritual ____test____.

> Jesus, full of the Holy Spirit, returned from the
> Jordan and was led by the Spirit in the desert, where
> for forty days he was tempted by the devil.
> **LUKE 4:1-2, NIV**

- Temptation isn't always about your ____weakness____. Many times, temptation is about ____Mis using your strength____

> The temptations that come into your life are no different from what others experience. And God is faithful. He will keep the temptation from becoming so strong that you can't stand up against it. When you are tempted, he will show you a way out so that you will not give in to it.
>
> **1 CORINTHIANS 10:13, NLT**

SEVEN STEPS TO ESCAPE TEMPTATION

- **Step #1:** Get into the <u>Word of God</u>

You cannot say, "It is written," if you don't know what is written.

> I have hidden your word in my heart so that I might not sin against you.
>
> **PSALM 119:11, NIV**

- **Step #2:** Identify your <u>vulnerabilites</u>.

> Watch and pray so that you will not fall into temptation. The spirit is willing but the body is weak.
>
> **MATTHEW 26:41, NIV**

- <u>When</u> am I most tempted?

- <u>Where</u> am I most tempted?

- Who is <u>with me</u> when I'm most tempted?

- How do I ___feel___ before I'm tempted?
- **Step #3:** ___Plan___ what you're ___not___ going to do.

> Plan carefully what you do ... Avoid evil and walk
> straight ahead. Don't go one step off the right way.
> **PROVERBS 4:26-27, TEV**

Plan in advance to stay away from people, places, or circumstances that cause you to be vulnerable to temptation. If you don't want to get stung, stay away from the bees. Plan what you're not going to do, and then stick to your plan.

- **Step #4:** Guard your ___heart___.

Temptation is an inside job.

> Temptation comes from our own desires,
> which entice us and drag us away.
> **JAMES 1:14, NLT**

> Above all else, guard your heart, for it
> affects everything you do.
> **PROVERBS 4:23, NLT**

- **Step #5:** Pray for ___deliverance___.

spending more than I should.

> God is faithful. He will keep the temptation from becoming so strong that you can't stand up against it. When you are tempted, he will show you a way out so that you will not give in to it.
>
> **1 CORINTHIANS 10:13, NLT**

- **Step #6:** Refocus your _attention_ .

Whatever gets your attention gets you. The battle for sin always starts in your mind. The only way to win that battle and escape temptation is to change your focus and think about something else.

- **Step #7:** Find a _friend_ .

> Two are better than one because together they can work more effectively. If one of them falls down, the other can help his friend get up. But how tragic it is for the one who is all alone when he falls. There is no one to help him get up.
>
> **ECCLESIASTES 4:9-10, TEV/GW**

If we had more people in our lives to whom we could confess our temptations, we would have less need to confess our sins.

Discovery Questions

How do you feel about yourself when you are tempted?

_____

_____

_____

_____

How does God feel about you when you are tempted?

_____

_____

_____

How can temptation draw you closer to God instead of farther from God?

_____

_____

_____

_____

Jesus' only defense when He was tempted was the Word of God. Which verse from this session will you memorize this week? Be prepared to recite it in your next session.

_____

_____

_____

_____

Putting It Into Practice

Before your next group meeting, identify the temptation you face most often, and spend some time applying the Seven Steps to Escape Temptation.

Step 1: Get in the Word. Make a commitment to spend at least ten minutes a day reading your Bible. Ask a friend to hold you accountable or to partner with you in your daily devotions (see Step 7).

Step 2: Identify your vulnerabilities. Make an honest self-assessment of your vulnerabilities. Don't be afraid of this process. Remember, when you know the truth, "the truth will set you free" (John 8:32, NIV).

Step 3: Plan what you're not going to do. Plan what you will do to avoid people, places, and circumstances that trigger your vulnerabilities. Stick to your plan.

Step 4: Guard your heart. Your eyes and ears are the gateways to your heart. What can you do to "guard your heart" (Proverbs 4:23, NIV)?

Step 5: Pray for deliverance. Begin your day with a prayer for deliverance. As Jesus taught us to pray, "Lead us not into temptation, but deliver us from evil" (Matthew 6:13, NIV). Ask God to help you and give you strength.

Step 6: Refocus your attention. Begin now to think of a "go-to place" that you can refocus your attention on whenever you are tempted: an activity, a hobby, a project, etc.

Step 7: Find a friend. Who do you know that can be trusted? To find this kind of friend, you need to be this kind of friend.

Prayer Direction

Pray that God will help each of you take the steps to escape temptation.

Pray for your group's prayer requests. Be sure to record their requests on the Prayer and Praise Report on pages 60-61.

Diving Deeper

For your daily quiet time this week, read the following Scripture passages about Jesus' temptation.

Matthew 4:1-11; Mark 1:12-13; Luke 4:1-13

SESSION 3

JESUS' SUFFERING
AND
YOUR SUFFERING

||||| CATCHING UP

- Did anyone memorize the verse you selected in the last session?

  _____

  _____

  _____

  _____

- Come up with a creative new ending to this statement: When the going gets tough, the tough ...

  _____

  _____

  _____

  _____

||||| KEY VERSE

We also rejoice in our suffering because we know that suffering produces perseverance, perseverance character and character, hope.

ROMANS 5:3-4, NIV

||||| WATCH the video lesson now and take notes in your outline.

Jesus' Suffering and Your Suffering

> Jesus ... for the joy set before him endured
> the cross, scorning its shame.
> **HEBREWS 12:2, NIV**

Looked past the pain

> We also rejoice in our suffering because we
> <u>know</u> that suffering produces <u>perseverance</u>,
> perseverance <u>character</u> and character, <u>hope</u>.
> **ROMANS 5:3-4, NIV**

suffering is enevitable because we live in a broken world

- **Suffering produces** ~~perseverance~~ .

You can either <u>panic</u> or <u>persevere</u> when you are under pressure. Which one do you think God wants you to do?

> We don't want you to be uninformed, brothers, about the
> hardship we suffered in the province of Asia. We were
> under great pressure, far beyond our ability to endure so
> that we despaired even of life. Indeed in our hearts we felt
> the sentence of death. But this happened that we might
> not rely on ourselves but on God who raises the dead.
> **2 CORINTHIANS 1:8-9, NIV**

Paul learned that in his own ability he could not handle the stress of life. But he also learned that in God's power he could handle anything. How did he learn that lesson? Through the things he suffered.

> I can do all things through Christ who strengthens me.
> **PHILIPPIANS 4:13, NKJV**

- **Perseverance produces** <u>character</u> *(of Jesus in me)* .

Tested and found realiable — Mettal puirified by fire.

> Consider it pure joy whenever you face trials of many kinds, because you know the testing of your faith develops perseverance. Perseverance must finish its work so that you may be mature and complete, not lacking anything.
> **JAMES 1:2-4, NIV**

- **Character produces** *Maturity hope.*

When you go through suffering, you can face it with resentment or gratitude; with complaining or rejoicing; with worry or worship; with fear or faith; with self-dependence or self-surrender.

When you ask God "Why?" and demand an explanation, you're not really looking for an answer. You're looking for an argument. Instead of saying "God, why are You doing this to me?" you should say what Jesus said: Father, not My will, but Your will be done (see Luke 22:42). Do whatever it takes to make me like Jesus in this trial I'm facing. My life is in Your hands.

Discovery Questions

If a friend of yours were going through a hard time and asked you, "If God loves me, why is He allowing me to suffer," how would you answer that question?

_____

_____

_____

_____

_____

_____

_____

_____

What problem in your life has caused the greatest growth in your character?

_____

_____

_____

_____

_____

_____

_____

_____

Are you more prone to pray "comfort me" prayers or "conform me" prayers? What is the difference between the two?

_____

_____

_____

_____

_____

_____

_____

_____

Are you currently experiencing hardship? If so, how is it affecting your relationship with God?

_____

_____

_____

_____

_____

_____

_____

_____

Putting It Into Practice

What challenge or difficulty are you facing right now? What do you think God wants you to learn? The most difficult prayer to pray is "Not my will, but Your will be done." Every day between now and your next session, ask God to have His will in every aspect of your life.

Select a Scripture verse from the message outline that you will memorize this week. Be prepared to recite it in your next session.

Prayer Direction

1 Thessalonians 5:18 (NLT) says, "Be thankful in all circumstances, for this is God's will for you who belong to Christ Jesus." No matter how bleak your circumstances might be, there is always something for which you can be thankful. Begin your group prayer time by making a list of what you know to be true about God: He is faithful, He is kind, He is loving, etc. Then offer brief prayers of thanksgiving for who He is.

Pray for your group's prayer requests. Be sure to record their requests on the Prayer and Praise Report on pages 60-61.

Diving Deeper

For your daily quiet time this week, read the following Scripture passages about Jesus' betrayal and arrest at Gethsemane.

Matthew 26:14-75; Mark 14:27-72; Luke 22:1-71; John 18:1-27

Notes

Pray for Luke - seeds planted.

SESSION 4

JESUS' DEATH
AND
YOUR DEATH

CATCHING UP

- **Did anyone memorize the verse you selected in the last session?**

____

____

____

____

- **Does anyone have a story to share of how God has answered prayer in the last week?**

____

____

____

____

KEY VERSE

I have been crucified with Christ and I no longer live, but Christ lives in me. The life I live in the body, I live by faith in the Son of God, who loved me and gave his life for me.

GALATIANS 2:20, NIV

WATCH the video lesson now and take notes in your outline.

Jesus' Death and Your Death

- **Jesus had to die so that** _you could live_ .

> The payment for sin is death.
> **ROMANS 6:23, GW**

> For everyone has sinned; we all fall short
> of God's glorious standard.
> **ROMANS 3:23, NLT**

> Now my soul is troubled and distressed, and what shall I
> say? Father, save me from this hour of trial and agony? But
> it was for this very purpose that I have come to this hour.
> **JOHN 12:27, AMP**

> I did not come to judge the world, but to save it.
> **JOHN 12:47, NIV**

- **Jesus crucifixion shows us** _God's love_ .

Can you imagine loving somebody so much that you would give your own son to die in their place? But that's exactly what God did for you.

> For God so loved the world that he gave his
> only begotten Son, that whoever believes in him
> should not perish but have everlasting life.
> **JOHN 3:16, NKJV**

When they drove the nails through the hands of Jesus, they went straight into the heart of God.

> Christ sacrificed his life's blood to set us free,
> which means that our sins are now forgiven.
> **EPHESIANS 1:7, CEV**

It's not what you do that gets you into heaven. It's what Jesus did. It's all by grace. It's all God's gift to you. All you need to do is believe and receive.

> To all who received him, to those who believed in his
> name, he gave the right to become children of God.
> **JOHN 1:12, NIV**

> What a God we have! ... Because Jesus was raised from the
> dead, we've been given a brand new life and have everything to
> live for, including a future in heaven—and the future starts now.
> **1 PETER 1:3-4, MSG**

> Anyone who belongs to Christ has become a new
> person. The old life is gone; a new life has begun!
> **2 CORINTHIANS 5:17, NLT**

> I have been crucified with Christ and I no longer live, but
> Christ lives in me. The life I live in the body, I live by faith in
> the Son of God, who loved me and gave his life for me.
> **GALATIANS 2:20, NIV**

> We know that our old sinful selves were crucified with Christ so that sin might lose its power in our lives ... For when we died with Christ we were set free from the power of sin. And since we died with Christ, we know we will also live with him.
>
> **ROMANS 6:6-8, NLT**

> Count yourselves dead to sin but alive to God in Christ Jesus.
>
> **ROMANS 6:11, NIV**

> There is now no condemnation for those who are in Christ Jesus.
>
> **ROMANS 8:1, NIV**

- I ought to ___love Jesus___.

> We love him because he first loved us.
>
> **1 JOHN 4:19, NKJV**

- I ought to ___hate sin___.

Sin is not a laughing matter. Just look at the cross.

- I ought to ___tell others___.

> God was in Christ, reconciling the world to himself, no longer counting peoples' sins against them. This is the wonderful message he has given us to tell others.
>
> **2 CORINTHIANS 5:19, NLT**

You're going to heaven because somebody told you about Jesus Christ. Is anybody going to be in heaven because of you?

Discovery Questions

How do you respond to the truth that your sins put Jesus on the cross?

_____

_____

_____

_____

What does it mean to you to be forgiven?

_____

_____

_____

_____

What does Jesus' conversation with the thief on the cross tell you about grace, salvation, and eternal life (see Luke 23:39-43)?

_____

_____

_____

_____

When Jesus was crucified, the sky grew dark, there was a violent earthquake, and the curtain in the temple was torn from top to bottom (see Matthew 27:45-53). What do you think all of that meant?

_____

_____

_____

_____

Putting It Into Practice

Every day this week, read 2 Corinthians 5:17, Galatians 2:20, Romans 6:6-8, Romans 6:1, and Romans 8:1 in your message outline. How should these truths affect your daily life? Make a list of all of the benefits that are promised in these verses.

_____

_____

_____

_____

_____

_____

Select a Scripture verse from the message outline that you will memorize this week. Be prepared to recite it in your next session.

Prayer Direction

Before sharing your prayer requests, take a few minutes in prayer to thank Jesus Christ for dying for you.

Pray for your group's prayer requests. Be sure to record their requests on the Prayer and Praise Report on pages 60-61.

Diving Deeper

For your daily quiet time this week, read the following Scripture passages about Jesus' crucifixion and burial.

Matthew 27:11-66; Mark 15:1-47; Luke 23:1-56; John 18:28-19:42

Notes

_____

_____

_____

_____

_____

_____

_____

_____

_____

_____

_____

_____

_____

_____

_____

_____

_____

_____

_____

_____

_____

_____

SON of GOD
The Life of Jesus in You

Session 5

JESUS' RESURRECTION
AND
YOUR RESURRECTION

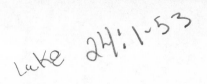
Luke 24:1-53

⦀ CATCHING UP

- Did anyone memorize the verse you selected in the last session?

  _____

  _____

  _____

  _____

- Before we begin our study of the resurrection, let's review some of the key promises that are ours because of Jesus' crucifixion. Turn to pages 32-34 in your study guide and read all of the Scripture verses in the message outline for session four.

  _____

  _____

  _____

⦀ KEY VERSE

And if the Spirit of him who raised Jesus from the dead is living in you, he who raised Christ from the dead will also give life to your mortal bodies through his Spirit, who lives in you.

ROMANS 8:11, NIV

⦀ **WATCH** the video lesson now and take notes in your outline.

Jesus' Resurrection and Your Resurrection

- **Jesus' resurrection shows us God's** <u>power</u>.

> [Jesus] showed himself alive to [his disciples] after his passion by many demonstrations: for forty days he continued to appear to them and tell them about the kingdom of God.
>
> **ACTS 1:3, NJB**

> By being raised from the dead he was proved to be the mighty Son of God, with the holy nature of God himself.
>
> **ROMANS 1:4, TLB**

- **Jesus' resurrection proves that** <u>He is God</u>.

> I pray that you will begin to understand how incredibly great his power is to help those who believe him. It is that same mighty power that raised Christ from the dead.
>
> **EPHESIANS 1:19-20, TLB**

> And if the Spirit of him who raised Jesus from the dead is living in you, he who raised Christ from the dead will also give life to your mortal bodies through his Spirit, who lives in you.
>
> **ROMANS 8:11, NIV**

The power of the resurrection is available to you when you give your life to Jesus Christ.

> It will happen in a moment, in the blink of an eye, when
> the last trumpet is blown. For when the trumpet sounds,
> those who have died will be raised to live forever.
> And we who are living will also be transformed.
> **1 CORINTHIANS 15:52, NLT**

That's the future hope of the resurrection. But in the meantime, while we wait for that day, what does the resurrection mean for us right here and now?

- **The power of the resurrection is the power to** _start over_

It's not a restart on your old life. It's a fresh start on a brand new life.

> Anyone who belongs to Christ is a new person.
> The past is forgotten, and everything is new.
> **2 CORINTHIANS 5:17, CEV**

> I will bestow on you a crown of beauty instead of ashes.
> **ISAIAH 61:3, NIV**

> I will restore to you the years that the
> swarming locust has eaten.
> **JOEL 2:25, NKJV**

God can make your life a new life, your home a new home, your marriage a new marriage, your heart a new heart, your mind a new mind. The power of the resurrection is the power to start over.

- **The power of the resurrection is the power to** _Keep going_ .

Jesus Christ gives you not only starting power, He gives you staying power. It's the power of persistence.

> I can do all things through Christ who strengthens me.
> **PHILIPPIANS 4:13, NKJV**

> Cast all your care upon him, for he cares for you.
> **1 PETER 5:7, NKJV**

If your problem is big enough to worry about, then it's big enough to pray about. Cast all your cares upon Him.

- **The power of the resurrection is the power to** _finish life successfully_ .

You don't need Jesus Christ just because you might die tonight. You need Jesus Christ because you have to live tomorrow. You need the power of the resurrection.

Because of the resurrection ...

- You can have _new life_ .
- You can have _an abundant life_ .

> I have come that you may have life, and that
> you may have it more <u>abundantly</u>.
> **JOHN 10:10, NKJV**

- You can have _eternal life_ .

Redeeming Love
Francine Rivers

Laurie- son Steven -
Applying for Special Ed
Job-

Luke Kathy
Katie
Christ

...nise
...ring Dad
...ck ...ome.

Discovery Questions

Why is Jesus' resurrection necessary for our salvation?

_____

_____

_____

Ephesians 1:19-20 and Romans 8:11 (see the message outline) teach us
that the power of God that raised Jesus from the dead is the same power
He uses to transform people's lives. Talk about the transformation that
has taken place in your life because of the death and resurrection of
Jesus Christ.

_____

_____

_____

...thy- M
...on Brian
home

The power of the resurrection is the power to start over, to keep going, and
to finish life confidently. Where do you need to see resurrection power at
work in your life right now?

_____

_____

_____

Your life on earth is preparation for eternity. Because of Jesus' resurrection,
you have the promise of eternal life. How should that truth affect the way
you live?

_____

_____

_____

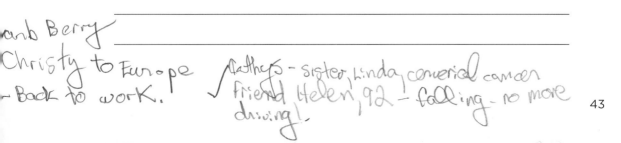

...anb Berry
Christy to Europe
- Back to work.

Mothers - sister, Linda converied cancer
friend Helen, 92 - falling - no more
driving!

Putting It Into Practice

Let's go back to the third discovery question: "The power of the resurrection is the power to start over, to keep going, and to finish life confidently. Where do you need to see resurrection power at work in your life right now?" Write down a change you want to see in your life, such as a habit, a thought pattern, a conflicted relationship, etc. What would "resurrection power" look like in that area of your life? What can you do to prepare the way for the Lord to change your heart and mind? What do you need to start believing or stop believing?

_____

_____

_____

_____

_____

Select a Scripture verse from the message outline that you will memorize this week. Be prepared to recite it in your next session.

Prayer Direction

Take a few minutes to thank God for the resurrection of Jesus Christ and for all that the power of the resurrection means to you.

"Cast all your care upon him, for he cares for you" (1 Peter 5:7, NKJV). Pray for your group's prayer requests. Be sure to record their requests on the Prayer and Praise Report on pages 60-61.

Diving Deeper

For your daily quiet time this week, read the following Scripture passages about Jesus' resurrection.

Matthew 28:1-20; Mark 16:1-20; Luke 24:1-53; John 20:1-31; Acts 1:3-9; 1 Corinthians 15:1-58

Notes

SESSION 6

JESUS' MINISTRY AND YOUR MINISTRY

IIIII CATCHING UP

- How did the truths you discussed in your last session about resurrection life affect your outlook this week?

_____

_____

_____

_____

- Did anyone memorize the verse you selected in the last session?

_____

_____

_____

_____

IIIII KEY VERSE

We are God's work of art, created in Christ Jesus
for the good works which God has already
designated to make up our way of life.

EPHESIANS 2:10, NJB

IIIII **WATCH** the video lesson now and take notes in your outline.

Jesus' Ministry and Your Ministry

> We are God's work of art, created in Christ Jesus
> for the good works which God has already
> designated to make up our way of life.
>
> **EPHESIANS 2:10, NJB**

> I tell you the truth, anyone who believes in me will
> do the same works I have done, and even greater
> works, because I am going to be with the Father.
>
> **JOHN 14:12, NLT**

> The Spirit of the Lord is on me, because he has anointed
> me to preach good news to the poor. He has sent me
> to heal the brokenhearted, to proclaim freedom for the
> prisoners and recovery of sight for the blind, to release
> the oppressed, to proclaim the year of the Lord's favor.
>
> **LUKE 4:18-19, NIV/NKJV**

- **Jesus came to** _____
  to the poor.

These are people who live with material poverty, moral poverty, or spiritual poverty.

Who do I know that needs the good news?

_____
Name

- **Jesus came to** _____ **the brokenhearted.**

These are people who are weighed down with disappointment, discouragement, defeat, or despair.

Who do I know that is hurting?

_____
Name

- Jesus came to _____ for those who are imprisoned.

These are people who are trapped by their circumstances, addictions, habits, or fears.

Who do I know that feels trapped?

_____
Name

- Jesus came to _____ to the blind.

These are people who are blind to the truth about God or about themselves.

Who do I know that is blind to the truth?

_____
Name

- Jesus came to _____ the oppressed.

These are people who are picked on, put down, victimized, or taken for granted.

Who do I know that is oppressed?

_____
Name

Jesus wants you to carry on His ministry to the world around you. He wants it to be your way of life.

Discovery Questions

Read Ephesians 2:10 in your message outline. The Bible says you are "God's work of art." How does that affect your self-perception?

_____

_____

_____

_____

Ephesians 2:10 also says that God has already designated good works to become "our way of life." What does that mean? How does that happen?

_____

_____

_____

_____

Look again at the five things Jesus was called to do. Which one resonates most with you? Which is the most challenging for you?

_____

_____

_____

_____

In John 14:12, Jesus said that we who believe in Him will do "even greater works" than He did because He was "going to be with the Father." What do you think He meant by that?

_____

_____

_____

_____

Putting It Into Practice

Think about the people whose names you wrote down. What opportunities for ministry are right in front of you? What do you think Jesus wants you to do? Make a plan to reach out to at least one of those people this week. It could be through a phone call, an email or text, or better yet, a personal visit. Plan what you will do, when you will do it, and how you will do it. Then stick to your plan. Ask a member of your small group to hold you accountable.

What will you do? _____

When will you do it? _____

How will you do it? _____

Select a Scripture verse from the message outline that you will memorize this week.

Prayer Direction

Take a few minutes to thank God for the lessons you have learned through this small group series.

Ask God to use you to carry on Jesus' ministry in the world around you. Pray for the people whose names you wrote down.

Pray for your group's prayer requests. Be sure to record their requests on the Prayer and Praise Report on pages 60-61.

Diving Deeper

For your daily quiet time this week, read the Gospel of Matthew to understand the full scope of Jesus' ministry.

Pastor Rick would love to hear how this study has impacted your life. You can write to him at *pastorrick@saddleback.com*.

For information about additional video based small-group studies from Pastor Rick Warren and Saddleback church, and to sign up for *Daily Hope*, Pastor Rick's freely daily devotional email, please *visit www.rickwarren.org*.

Notes

SMALL-GROUP RESOURCES

HELPS FOR HOSTS
Top Ten Ideas for New Hosts

Congratulations. As the host of your small group, you have responded to the call to help shepherd Jesus' flock. Few other tasks in the family of God surpass the contribution you will be making. As you prepare to facilitate your group, whether it is one session or the entire series, here are a few additional thoughts to keep in mind. We encourage you to read and review these tips with each new discussion host before he or she leads.

Remember you are not alone. God knows everything about you, and he knew you would be asked to facilitate your group. Even though you may not feel ready, this is common for all good hosts. God promises, "I will never leave you; I will never abandon you" (Hebrews 13:5, TEV). Whether you are facilitating for one evening, several weeks, or a lifetime, you will be blessed as you serve.

1. Don't try to do it alone. Pray right now for God to help you build a healthy team. If you can enlist a co-host to help you shepherd the group, you will find your experience much richer. This is your chance to involve as many people as you can in building a healthy group. All you have to do is ask people to help. You'll be surprised at their response.

2. Be friendly and be yourself. God wants to use your unique gifts and temperament. Be sure to greet people at the door with a big smile. This can set the mood for the whole gathering. Remember, they are taking as big a step to show up at your house as you are to host a small group! Don't try to do things exactly like another host; do them in a way that fits you. Admit when you don't have an answer and apologize when you make a mistake. Your group will love you for it and you'll sleep better at night.

3. Prepare for your meeting ahead of time. Review the session and write down your responses to each question. Pay special attention to "Putting It Into Practice" exercises that ask group members to do something other than engage in discussion. These exercises will help your group live what the Bible teaches, not just talk about it.

4. Pray for your group members by name. Before your group arrives, take a few moments to pray for each member by name. You may want to review the Small-Group Prayer and Praise Report on page 60-61 at least once a week. Ask God to use your time together to touch the heart of every person in your group. Expect God to lead you to whomever he wants you to encourage or challenge in a special way. If you listen, God will surely lead.

5. When you ask a question, be patient. Someone will eventually respond. Sometimes people need a moment or two of silence to think about the question. If silence doesn't bother you, it won't bother anyone else. After someone responds, affirm the response with a simple "thanks" or "great answer." Then ask, "How about somebody else?" or "Would someone who hasn't shared like to add anything?" Be sensitive to new people or members who are reluctant to say, pray, or do anything. If you give them a safe setting, they will blossom over time. If someone in your group is a wallflower who sits silently through every session, consider talking to them privately and encouraging them to participate. Let them know how important they are to you—that they are loved and appreciated, and that the group would value their input. Remember, still water often runs deep.

6. Provide transitions between questions. Ask if anyone would like to read the question or Bible passage. Don't call on anyone, but ask for a volunteer, and then be patient until someone begins. Be sure to thank the person who reads aloud.

7. Break into smaller groups occasionally. This is especially helpful if your group has more than ten members. With a greater opportunity to talk in a small circle, people will connect more with the study, apply more quickly what they're learning, and ultimately get more out of their small-group experience. A small circle also encourages a quiet person to participate and tends to minimize the effects of a more vocal or dominant member.

8. Small circles are also helpful during prayer time. People who are unaccustomed to praying aloud will feel more comfortable trying it with just two or three others. Also, prayer requests won't take as much time, so circles will have more time to actually pray. When you gather back with the whole group, you can have one person from each circle briefly update everyone on the prayer requests from their sub-groups. The other great aspect of sub-grouping is that it fosters leadership development. As you ask people in the group to facilitate discussion or to lead a prayer circle, it gives them a small leadership step that can build their confidence.

9. Rotate facilitators occasionally. You may be perfectly capable of hosting each time, but you will help others grow in their faith and gifts if you give them opportunities to host the group.

10. One final challenge (for new or first-time hosts): Before your first opportunity to lead, look up each of the six passages listed on the next page. Read each one as a devotional exercise to help prepare you with a shepherd's heart. Trust us on this one. If you do this, you will be more than ready for your first meeting.

When Jesus saw the crowds, he had compassion on them, because they were harassed and helpless, like sheep without a shepherd. Then he said to his disciples, "The harvest is plentiful but the workers are few. Ask the Lord of the harvest, therefore, to send out workers into his harvest field."
MATTHEW 9:36-38, NIV

I am the good shepherd; I know my sheep and my sheep know me—just as the Father knows me and I know the Father—and I lay down my life for the sheep.
JOHN 10:14-15, NIV

Be shepherds of God's flock that is under your care, serving as overseers—not because you must, but because you are willing, as God wants you to be; not greedy for money, but eager to serve; not lording it over those entrusted to you, but being examples to the flock. And when the Chief Shepherd appears, you will receive the crown of glory that will never fade away.
1 PETER 5:2-4, NIV

If you have any encouragement from being united with Christ, if any comfort from his love, if any fellowship with the Spirit, if any tenderness and compassion, then make my joy complete by being like-minded, having the same love, being one in spirit and purpose. Do nothing out of selfish ambition or vain conceit, but in humility consider others better than yourselves. Each of you should look not only to your own interests, but also to the interests of others. Your attitude should be the same as that of Jesus Christ.
PHILIPPIANS 2:1-5, NIV

Let us hold unswervingly to the hope we profess, for he who promised is faithful. And let us consider how we may spur one another on toward love and good deeds. Let us not give up meeting together, as some are in the habit of doing, but let us encourage one another—and all the more as you see the Day approaching.
HEBREWS 10:23-25, NIV

But we were gentle among you, like a mother caring for her little children. We loved you so much that we were delighted to share with you not only the Gospel of God but our lives as well, because you had become so dear to us ... For you know that we dealt with each of you as a father deals with his own children, encouraging, comforting and urging you to live lives worthy of God, who calls you into his kingdom and glory.
1 THESSALONIANS 2:7,8, 11–12, NIV

FREQUENTLY ASKED QUESTIONS

HOW LONG WILL THIS GROUP MEET? This small-group study is six sessions long. We encourage your group to add a seventh session for a celebration. In your final session, each group member may decide if he or she desires to continue with the group for another study. At that time you may also want to do some informal evaluation, discuss your Small-Group Guidelines (see page 58), and decide which study you want to do next. We recommend you visit our website at *www.rickwarren.org* for more video-based small-group studies.

WHO IS THE HOST? The host is the person who coordinates and facilitates your group meetings. In addition to a host, we encourage you to select one or more group members to lead your group discussions. Several other responsibilities can be rotated, including refreshments, prayer requests, worship, or keeping up with members who miss a meeting. Shared ownership in the group helps everybody grow.

WHERE DO WE FIND NEW GROUP MEMBERS? Recruiting new members can be a challenge for groups, especially new groups with just a few people, or existing groups that lose a few people along the way. We encourage you to use the Circles of Life diagram on page 57 of this study guide to brainstorm a list of people from your workplace, church, school, neighborhood, family, and so on. Then pray for the people on each member's list. Allow each member to invite several people from their list. Some groups fear that newcomers will interrupt the intimacy that members have built over time. However, groups that welcome newcomers generally gain strength with the infusion of new blood. Remember, the next person you add just might become a friend for eternity. Logistically, groups find different ways to add members. Some groups remain permanently open, while others choose to open periodically, such as at the beginning or end of a study. If your group becomes too large for easy, face-to-face conversations, you can sub-group, forming a second discussion group in another room.

HOW DO WE HANDLE THE CHILD-CARE NEEDS IN OUR GROUP?
Child-care needs must be handled very carefully. This is a sensitive issue. We suggest you seek creative solutions as a group. One common solution is to have the adults meet in the living room and share the cost of a babysitter (or two) who can be with the kids in another part of the house. Another popular option is to have one home for the kids and a second home (close by) for the adults. If desired, the adults could rotate the responsibility of providing a lesson for the kids. This last option is great with school age kids and can be a huge blessing to families.

CIRCLES OF LIFE: SMALL-GROUP CONNECTIONS

Discover who you can connect in community

Use this chart to help carry out one of the values in the
Small-Group Guidelines, to "Welcome Newcomers."

Follow me, and I will make you fishers of men.
MATTHEW 4:19, KJV

Family
(immediate or
extended)

_____

_____

Fellowship   **Friends**
(church   (neighbors, kids,
relationships)   sports, school, etc.)

_____   _____

_____   _____

Fun   **Factory/Firm**
(gym, hobbies,   (work,
hang-outs)   professional arenas)

_____   _____

_____   _____

Follow this simple three-step process:

1. List one or two people in each circle.

2. Prayerfully select one person or couple from your list and tell your group about them.

3. Give them a call and invite them to your next meeting. Over fifty percent of those invited to a small group say, "Yes!"

SMALL-GROUP GUIDELINES

It's a good idea for every group to put words to their shared values, expectations, and commitments. Such guidelines will help you avoid unspoken agendas and unmet expectations. We recommend you discuss your guidelines during Session One in order to lay the foundation for a healthy group experience. Feel free to modify anything that does not work for your group.

We agree to the following VALUES:

CLEAR PURPOSE

To grow healthy spiritual lives by building a healthy small-group community

GROUP ATTENDANCE

To give priority to the group meeting (call if I am absent or late)

SAFE ENVIRONMENT

To create a safe place where people can be heard and feel loved (no quick answers, snap judgments, or simple fixes)

BE CONFIDENTIAL

To keep anything that is shared strictly confidential and within the group

CONFLICT RESOLUTION

To avoid gossip and to immediately resolve any concerns by following the principles of Matthew 18:15-17

SPIRITUAL HEALTH

To give group members permission to speak into my life and help me live a healthy, balanced spiritual life that is pleasing to God

LIMIT OUR FREEDOM

To limit our freedom by not serving or consuming alcohol during small-group meetings or events so as to avoid causing a weaker brother or sister to stumble (1 Corinthians 8:1-13; Romans 14:19-21)

WELCOME NEWCOMERS

To invite friends who might benefit from this study and warmly welcome newcomers

BUILDING RELATIONSHIPS

To get to know the other members of the group and pray for them regularly

OTHER

_____

_____

_____

_____

We have also discussed and agree on the following items:

CHILD CARE

_____

_____

_____

STARTING TIME

_____

ENDING TIME

_____

If you haven't already done so, take a few minutes to fill out the Small-Group Calendar on page 62 and the Small-Group Roster on page 64.

SMALL-GROUP PRAYER AND PRAISE REPORT

This is a place where you can write each other's requests for prayer. You can also make a note when God answers a prayer. Pray for each other's requests. If you're new to group prayer, it's okay to pray silently or to pray by using just one sentence:

"God, please help _____ to _____."

DATE	PERSON	PRAYER REQUEST	PRAISE REPORT

DATE	PERSON	PRAYER REQUEST	PRAISE REPORT

SMALL-GROUP CALENDAR

Healthy groups share responsibilities and group ownership. It might take some time for this to develop. Shared ownership ensures that responsibility for the group doesn't fall to one person. Use the calendar to keep track of social events, mission projects, birthdays, or days off. Complete this calendar at your first or second meeting. Planning ahead will increase attendance and shared ownership.

DATE	LESSON	LOCATION	FACILITATOR	SNACK OR MEAL
10/22	Session 2	Steve & Laura	Bill Jones	John & Alice

Answer Key

SESSION ONE

- You need to be baptized because Jesus <u>demonstrated</u> it.
- You need to be baptized because Jesus <u>commanded</u> it.
- Baptism is your <u>public statement</u> that you belong to Jesus Christ.
- Baptism is a symbol of <u>incorporation</u>.

SESSION TWO

- It is not a <u>sin</u> to be tempted.
- You will never <u>outgrow</u> temptation.
- After a spiritual <u>high</u>, you can expect a spiritual <u>test</u>.
- Temptation isn't always about your <u>weaknesses</u>. Many times, temptation is about <u>misusing your strengths</u>.
- Step #1: Get into the <u>Word</u>.
- Step #2: Identify your <u>vulnerabilities</u>.
  - <u>When</u> am I most tempted?
  - <u>Where</u> am I most tempted?
  - Who is <u>with me</u> when I'm most tempted?
  - How do I <u>feel</u> before I'm tempted?
- Step #3: <u>Plan</u> what you're <u>not</u> going to do.
- Step #4: Guard your <u>heart</u>.
- Step #5: Pray for <u>deliverance</u>.
- Step #6: Refocus your <u>attention</u>.
- Step #7: Find a <u>friend</u>.

SESSION THREE

- Suffering produces <u>perseverance</u>.
- Perseverance produces <u>character</u>.
- Character produces <u>hope</u>.

SESSION FOUR

- Jesus had to die so that <u>you could live</u>.
- Jesus crucifixion shows us <u>God's love</u>.
- I ought to <u>love Christ</u>.
- I ought to <u>hate sin</u>.
- I ought to <u>tell others</u>.

SESSION FIVE

- Jesus' resurrection shows us God's <u>power</u>.
- Jesus' resurrection proves that <u>He is God</u>.
- The power of the resurrection is the power to <u>start over</u>.
- The power of the resurrection is the power to <u>keep going</u>.
- The power of the resurrection is the power to <u>finish life confidently</u>.
- You can have <u>a new life</u>.
- You can have <u>an abundant life</u>.
- You can have <u>eternal life</u>.

SESSION SIX

- Jesus came to <u>preach the good news</u> to the poor.
- Jesus came to <u>comfort</u> the brokenhearted.
- Jesus came to <u>proclaim freedom</u> for those who are imprisoned.
- Jesus came to <u>recover sight</u> to the blind.
- Jesus came to <u>release</u> the oppressed.

SMALL-GROUP ROSTER

NAME	EMAIL	PHONE